What You Should Know About... Inventions

Table of Contents

by Nancy White

What You Should Know About . . . SERIES

The Truth About Inventions

Was the wheel invented by early humans? No—and it wasn't invented to help people get around either. What about blue jeans? Were they invented by a fashion designer? No, again. The original jeans were made more than 100 years ago for men doing hard and heavy work. And if you think the first computer was a desktop, think again.

Unexpected facts often turn up when you find out the origins of the things we use, wear, and eat. You may know some of these facts already, but many of them are guaranteed to surprise you.

Many inventions sound crazy at first. But inventors have always relied on their imaginations to "think outside the box" without worrying about making mistakes or looking foolish. From the wheel to the World Wide Web, inventions have solved problems, changed the way people live, and even changed the course of history. Whenever you have a problem to solve, let yourself be inspired by the people who came up with the original ideas in this book. You may be surprised at where your imagination will take you.

A Tale of Spaghetti

Many people believe that spaghetti, the popular Italian food, was invented in China and brought to Italy by Marco Polo. Marco Polo was a **legendary** Italian traveler who wrote about his travels to China in the thirteenth century. Historians are not sure how much of what Marco Polo wrote is fact and how much is fiction. Polo may have brought Chinese inventions such as the compass and paper money back to Europe. However, he did not discover spaghetti in China.

Some historians think that spaghetti was invented right where you would expect—in Italy. An ancient book written 100 years before Marco Polo was born suggests spaghetti was invented in Sicily, a large Italian island in the Mediterranean Sea.

Spaghetti is an ancient invention.

The ancient book was written by a geographer and historian who was **commissioned** by Sicily's ruler, King Roger II, to write about Sicily. The book is known as *The Book of Roger*. It mentions that people living in the Sicilian town of Trabia made a paste out of wheat, shaped it into long strands, and dried it. The food isn't called *spaghetti* in the book, but it sure sounds like it.

Even if spaghetti wasn't actually invented in Sicily, it was made not far away. We know this because the kind of wheat used for spaghetti grew only around the Mediterranean at that time. It did not grow in China.

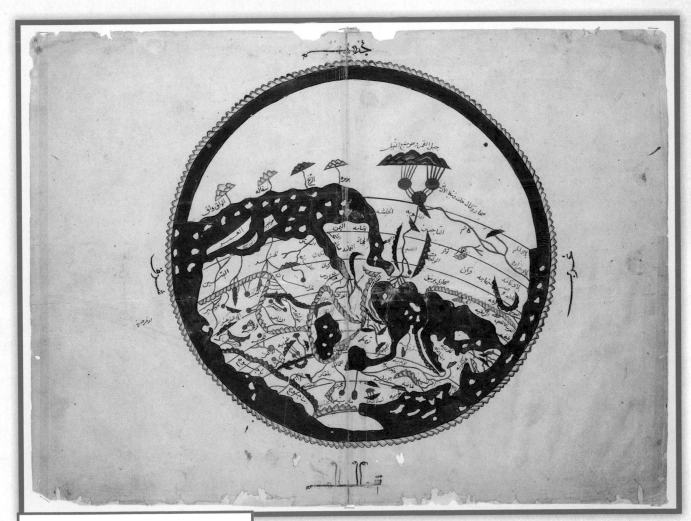

A page from *The Book of Roger*

The Source of Silk

Spaghetti probably wasn't invented in China, but many other things were, including silk. According to legend, a Chinese princess discovered silk more than 4,500 years ago. Princess Hsi Ling Shih was enjoying a cup of tea outdoors when a puffy white cocoon plopped into her tea from a tree branch above her. Naturally, she removed it from her drink. As she pulled out the cocoon, however, it began to unravel in her fingers. The princess discovered that the cocoon was made of a beautiful smooth, yet tough, thread. Hsi Ling Shih decided to raise the worms that made the cocoons and weave their threads into a new fabric: silk.

The worms were wrinkly, hairless, and blind, but their thread was gorgeous and shiny. Each cocoon produced about a thousand yards (one kilometer) of thread! At first only the emperor and his closest family and friends were allowed to wear the valuable fabric, and the secret to making silk was guarded fiercely. The emperor warned that anyone who breathed a word about the magic of silkworms would be punished by death.

For almost 3,000 years, the Chinese succeeded in keeping the secret of silk from most of the world. They sold their luxurious fabric around Asia and Europe by camel and yak, using well-traveled trading routes known as the Silk Road. Silk continued to grow more popular, and curiosity about how it was made grew stronger. As Chinese people began to travel more widely, the secret became harder and harder to keep.

After years of rumors, people in Europe and elsewhere finally pieced together the incredible truth about the mysterious fabric. They learned that silkworms snack on mulberry tree leaves day and night, multiplying their body weight 10,000 times in a month. Once they're full to bursting, the worms begin to spin cocoons out of fine thread. After eight or nine days, the cocoons are steamed or baked, and the thread is unraveled and woven into silk.

Once the secret was out, it was just a matter of time before silkworm eggs were smuggled out of China. One person hid the eggs in a hairpiece, and a couple of monks hid some in their hollow bamboo canes. At last, the world knew the secret of silk, a fabric still admired for its beauty and strength today.

Silk was invented
around 2640 B.C.E.

The Wright Brothers Take Flight

On December 17, 1903, the Wright Flyer, invented and built by Orville and Wilbur Wright, flew over Kitty Hawk, North Carolina, U.S.A. The flight covered a distance of 120 feet (37 meters) and lasted for 12 seconds.

Many inventors before the Wrights made aircraft that could fly. However, the Wright brothers get credit for the airplane because their invention was the first to combine all three of the following features:

A Motor The Wright Flyer had a small engine that used gasoline. Many of the earlier flying machines were **gliders**. A glider has wings to hold it up, but no motor to get it off the ground or keep it going. To take off, a glider has to be pushed off a high cliff or pulled along the ground until it lifts. Then, it flies by floating on air currents.

The Wright Flyer in 1903

8

Heavier than Air Previously, aircraft filled with hot air or a gas that is lighter than air, such as hydrogen, had made successful flights. The first lighter-than-air craft was the hot-air balloon, invented in 1783 by another pair of brothers—the Montgolfiers from France. In 1852, another Frenchman, Henri Giffard, flew a **dirigible**, a lighter-than-air craft similar to a blimp, 17 miles (27.35 kilometers) at 5 miles (8 kilometers) per hour.

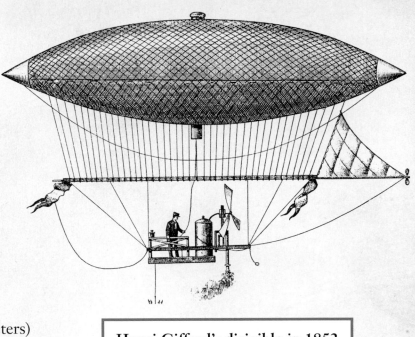

Henri Giffard's dirigible in 1852

A Pilot Some earlier experimental aircraft were not considered safe enough to carry a person. The third reason the Wrights get credit for inventing the airplane is that the Wright Flyer carried a pilot. His name was Orville Wright.

The True Father of Flight

Probably the first person to seriously consider the possibility of human flight was Leonardo da Vinci, the brilliant Italian artist and inventor. In 1485—more than 400 years before the Wright brothers—Leonardo drew plans for mechanical wings that would allow a person to fly. He also made plans for a glider.

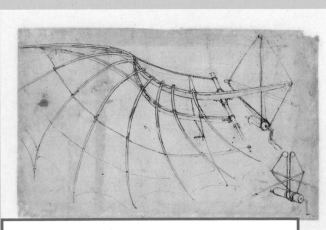

Leonardo da Vinci's drawing of a mechanical wing from around 1485 C.E.

9

Baseball's International Past

Today's rules for baseball were invented in America. However, many common beliefs about America's national pastime are not true. Here are just a few examples:

1. True or False? Baseball is 100 percent American.
Answer: False. There are older games from England, such as cricket and rounders, that use bats and balls. They are the ancestors of American baseball.

2. True or False? Baseball was first played in 1839.
Answer: False. Americans were playing baseball before 1839, but the players made up their own rules.

3. True or False? Baseball was invented by Abner Doubleday.
Answer: False. This claim was made in 1905 by a man who said he witnessed Doubleday invent the game back in 1839. But Doubleday actually had nothing to do with baseball—the story was completely made up. Doubleday was an officer in the U.S. Army, and he would have denied the claim himself— if he had not died nearly fifteen years before.

4. True or False? Alexander Cartwright was the "father of American baseball."

Answer: False. Cartwright did contribute to the game. For example, he made a rule against getting runners out by throwing the ball at them. However, even more credit should go to several other people, including Daniel ("Doc") Adams and Louis Wadsworth. Adams set the bases ninety feet (27.5 meters) apart and created the position of **shortstop**. It was probably Wadsworth who decided that there would be nine players on a team and nine innings in a game.

So yes, baseball is an American game, but it has an international history and more than one inventor. Perhaps we should say that baseball was developed and not even use the word *invented*!

This photo from 1858 shows two rival baseball teams—the New York Knickerbockers and the Brooklyn Excelsiors. The man dressed as Abe Lincoln is the umpire.

Bicycles Without Pedals

Since the word *bicycle* means "two wheels," a wooden **contraption** from around 1790 can be considered the world's first bicycle. It had two wheels and a seat, but it lacked two other important features—pedals and handlebars. The rider sat on the seat and moved by walking or running along the ground, but the bike could only travel in a straight line. A French inventor named Comte Mede de Sivrac built the contraption and called it the *celerifere*. More than twenty years later, a German inventor named Baron Karl von Drais added handles for steering.

It wasn't until 1839 that Kirkpatrick Macmillan, a Scottish blacksmith, came up with a brilliant idea—pedals. They were attached to the front wheel. Unfortunately, Macmillan ran over a **pedestrian** with his new invention.

The French inventor Ernest Michaux [me-SHOW] also designed a pedaled bicycle. It was made of iron and had wooden wheels. No wonder it was nicknamed the boneshaker!

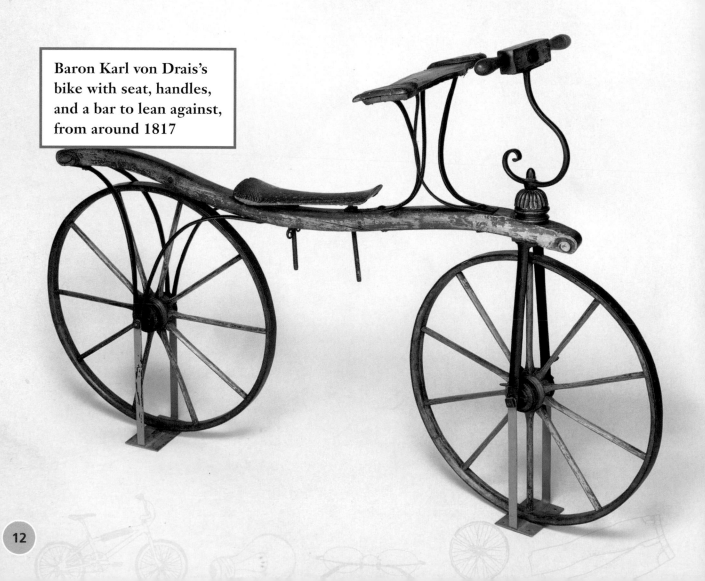

Baron Karl von Drais's bike with seat, handles, and a bar to lean against, from around 1817

John Kemp Starley's Rover Safety Bicycle from around 1885

Next came a less bone-shaking bicycle with a lighter frame and rubber wheels. The front wheel was much bigger than the rear wheel. It was a lot more comfortable to ride, but the problem with this bicycle was that the brakes didn't work very well.

Around 1885, British inventor John Kemp Starley produced the Rover Safety Bicycle. With two wheels the same size, inflatable tires, handlebars, brakes, pedals, and a chain, a time traveler from the twenty-first century would recognize the Rover as a bike. Even the frame was shaped like the frames of modern bicycles.

In the same way that the invention of the bicycle involved many inventors over many years, mountain bikes, racing bikes, and bikes with fifteen or more gears all came later. But John Kemp Starley deserves credit for being the "father of the modern bicycle."

The Rugged History of Jeans

Many people around the world wear jeans. You can buy them in all kinds of stores. You can even pay anywhere from a few dollars up to hundreds of dollars just for one pair. But jeans didn't start out that way.

The story of blue jeans starts with a young German-Jewish immigrant who moved with his family to New York City in the United States in 1847. His name was Levi Strauss. Levi and his two brothers owned a store in New York where they sold cloth. Then, in 1853, Levi headed out to San Francisco, California, U.S.A., to start his own business. Many people had moved to San Francisco to look for gold, and Levi wanted to sell cloth and other goods to them. Levi's business did well, and he became quite wealthy.

Levi Strauss was born in Germany on February 26, 1829. He died in San Francisco, California, U.S.A., on September 26, 1902.

One day, Levi received a letter from a customer named Jacob Davis. Davis was a tailor who had bought sturdy cloth from Levi's store and used it to make a new kind of pants that were very popular with farmers and gold miners. Working men liked the pants because the pocket seams were **reinforced** with copper **rivets**. Davis wanted to **patent** his invention, but he didn't have the money necessary to apply for a patent.

Levi and Davis each paid half of the money, and they became business partners. They called the pants Levi's. The rest is history! Levi's are just one of many brands of jeans today, but some people still refer to all jeans as Levi's.

What Is a Patent?

In the United States, a patent is a right given by the government to a person or group of people who have invented something new. A patented invention cannot be made or sold in the U.S. by anyone but the inventor. Most patents last for twenty years. Levi's were patented a long time ago on May 20, 1873, so now pants with copper rivets can be made by designers everywhere.

Marshmallows

The Egyptian queen Cleopatra might have eaten marshmallows. The white, squishy **confection** was invented by ancient Egyptians more than three thousand years ago. They thickened the candy with the sticky root of the marshmallow plant and sweetened it with honey. Modern marshmallows are thickened with gelatin and sweetened with sugar.

Marshmallows were invented in Egypt more than three thousand years ago.

Ketchup

Kachiap was a spicy sauce used hundreds of years ago in China and Malaysia. In the 1600s, traders brought the sauce to England. The English called it "catsup."

Next stop, America. In 1876, Henry John Heinz started selling his own version of the sauce, which tasted nothing like the original. He called it "ketchup." By 1907, he was producing 12 million bottles per year and exporting it all over the world.

Henry John Heinz was just one of the inventors of ketchup.

Mayonnaise

Mayonnaise was invented by a French chef in the 1700s. He made a rich sauce out of olive oil and egg yolks to serve at a fancy **banquet**. About two hundred years later, a man named Richard Hellmann started selling jars of mayonnaise in his store in New York City, U.S.A. Hellmann's mayonnaise is still popular in the United States, but "mayo" is more likely to be used on a sandwich than on a fancy dish at a dinner party.

How to make your own mayonnaise: Beat two egg yolks. Slowly add 1 cup of olive oil while you are still beating. Mix in 2 tablespoons of lemon juice.

Richard Hellmann started selling his mayonnaise in the early 1900s, but the sauce was actually invented in the 1700s.

Sandwich

The sandwich was named after an Englishman, John Montagu, the fourth Earl of Sandwich. It is said that around the year 1762, he told his cook to put some sliced meat between two pieces of bread so he could eat it quickly. A likely reason is that the Earl worked long hours at his desk, and needed something quick and easy to eat to keep himself going. Of course, he wasn't the first person to eat bread with meat or cheese, but the humble sandwich was named for this wealthy Englishman.

The sandwich, invented around 1762, remains vastly popular today.

The First Compasses

If you've ever gone camping or on a hike, you may have used a compass. It's a small device that shows you which way is north, to help you figure out your direction. Hundreds of years ago, the compass certainly helped sailors know where they were going. Before compasses, they did not have reliable ways of keeping track of their position and their course. One method was simply to stay close to shore and use familiar landmarks as guides. If they had to sail out of sight of land, they used the height of the sun or the position of the stars, moon, and planets to stay on course. Often, sailors relied on just plain guesswork.

The compass was invented in China sometime around 250 B.C.E. The first compass was a bronze disk with a spoon-shaped piece of **lodestone** placed on it. Because lodestone is magnetic, the bowl-shaped part of the spoon pointed toward the magnetic field of Earth's North Pole. The handle of the spoon always pointed south. The Chinese didn't use this compass to help ships **navigate**, but to determine the best location for burials.

The early lodestone compass would not have worked very well on a ship, because the rolling seas would have knocked the lodestone off the disk. It wasn't until 1100 C.E., another thousand years later, that the Chinese figured out how to replace the lodestone with something more stable: a magnetized needle. By rubbing a needle with a magnetic **mineral** called magnetite, they were able to make a more practical compass—one that allowed sailors to explore the world.

⊢ A Compass for Your House ⊢

In China and some other parts of the world, compasses are still used to determine the best and luckiest way to position houses, public buildings, and monuments. This practice, called *feng shui* [fung SWHAY], is also used to determine the most peaceful, comfortable, and relaxing way to arrange objects in a room.

This Chinese lodestone compass dates back to 220 B.C.E.

Ancient Wheels

The wheel seems like such a simple object that many people believe it must have been invented in prehistoric times. The inventors of the wheel weren't "cavemen," however. On the contrary, they were quite civilized. They wore clothes, played musical instruments, constructed buildings and towns, and made pottery. And that's where the wheel comes in.

Diagrams drawn on ancient clay tablets lead **archaeologists** to believe that the first wheels were not used for transportation, as most people think, but to make pottery. The tablets were found in Mesopotamia, the ancient area that is part of present-day Iraq, and date back to around 3500 B.C.E.

This work of art shows ancient Mesopotamian war chariots from around 2600 B.C.E.

Pottery was very important in the ancient world because people stored grain in it. Potters made large pots by coiling a piece of clay and winding the coil around and around, building it higher and higher. In order to do this, the potter had to keep walking around and around the pot.

Making pottery became easier and faster when someone had the idea to put the clay on a round disk and spin it. Instead of walking in circles, the potter could stand still and turn the disk. Thus the wheel was born, probably around 3500 B.C.E. It was another 300 years before the Mesopotamians figured out how to add wheels to a cart—and invent the chariot.

Making coiled pottery

The First Computers

None of the first computers could fit on a desk. For example, the ENIAC [EH-nee-ack], one of the world's earliest computers, weighed 30 tons (27 metric tons) and took up as much space as an average swimming pool or volleyball court. (That's 1,800 square feet, or 167 square meters.) It was designed in 1943, during World War II, to perform calculations that would help the U.S. Army fire bombs and other weapons more accurately. By the time the ENIAC was completed, the war was over, but the computer, which cost about $400,000 to build, didn't go to waste. It was used for ten years to do scientific research.

By the 1950s, other large computers were being built, but they were used only by governments and businesses. The president of a computer company was quoted as saying, "There is no reason for any individual to have a computer at home."

How wrong he was! Computers became smaller and smaller. During the 1970s the first personal computers, known as PCs, hit the market. They were finally small enough to fit on people's desktops. The first laptops came along in the 1980s.

Those computers would seem **primitive** to us now, to say nothing of hard to use. And they didn't have e-mail or the Internet. In fact, today's pocket-sized cell phones can do more than the enormous computers of the past like ENIAC.

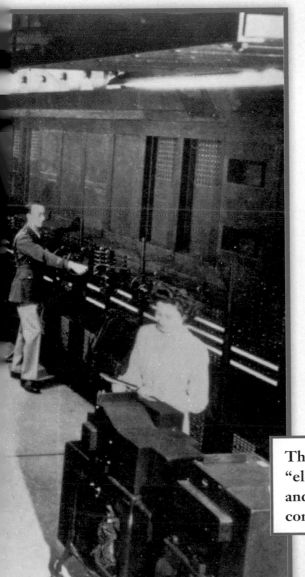

The letters ENIAC stood for "electronic numerical integrator and computer." The massive computer nearly filled this room.

Yesterday's Eyeglasses

"I can't find my glasses!" Anyone who wears glasses knows how awful those words are and how essential glasses can be. Even 1,000 years ago, people who had trouble seeing small things used a special piece of glass to see. It was called a reading stone—a **convex lens** that made letters and objects appear larger when viewed under it. Today, we call it a magnifying glass.

Historical writings show that the first eyeglasses were made in Italy around the year 1286. They were just two small reading stones, each surrounded by a frame with a small handle. The handles were connected so the wearer could hold the lenses in place or balance them on his or her nose.

This portrait was painted by an Italian artist in 1352. It shows a priest wearing eyeglasses as he works at his desk. Early glasses, such as the ones in the painting, had no earpieces. They balanced on the wearer's nose.

Eyeglasses became popular during the 1300s. By the 1400s, **concave** lenses for distance vision were also available.

After the printing press was invented around 1450, books became available to many more people. Glasses, also called spectacles or "specs," became even more popular because people wanted to read. (Before the printing press, books had been copi   d, which made them too expensive for most people to buy.)

G   ved over the centuries. They stay on better, for one thing!   lenses are made according to individual prescriptions,   tacts instead of "specs."

Looking Smart

During the fifteenth century, glasses became a sign of seriousness and intelligence. Artists sometimes painted glasses on people in portraits, just to make the people appear **scholarly**. The idea that glasses make people look smart has never really disappeared. Think of Harry Potter.

Inventors of the Lightbulb

Before the electric lightbulb, people lit up the dark with candles and lamps that burned gas. The American inventor Thomas Alva Edison is sometimes credited for the invention of the lightbulb, but he was far from the first person to think that electricity could do a better job at lighting a room than candles.

Many inventors came up with electric lights that worked, but they were not practical. For example, an Englishman named Warren de la Rue placed a thin strip of material called a **filament** inside a glass bulb. He used electricity to heat the filament until it was hot enough to glow and give off light. But the filament was made of the precious metal platinum, so the lightbulb was too expensive for ordinary people to use.

Thomas Edison shows a copy of his first successful lightbulb, which he perfected in 1879.

In 1878, an English scientist named Joseph Swan made an improved and less expensive lightbulb, but the filament burned out too quickly. In addition, as it burned, a layer of dark soot built up inside the glass bulb, dimming the light.

One or two years later, around 1880, Edison and his research team improved on Swan's invention by using a filament made out of carbonized bamboo. It was inexpensive and could burn continuously for more than 1,200 hours, or fifty days.

A Bright New Idea

Edison didn't invent the first lightbulb, and he didn't invent the last one either. Even though his bulbs were improved over the years, they're still inefficient. Less than six percent of the energy used by a lightbulb goes toward producing light. All the rest is given off as heat.

People who want to keep down their electricity bills and help keep the environment clean can buy compact fluorescent lamps (CFLs) instead. These bulbs convert electricity into light much more efficiently by using mercury vapor. CFLs use one-third the electricity and last ten times longer than the standard bulb. (If we replaced one regular bulb with a CFL in every household in the United States, it would have the same effect on the environment as taking 7.5 million cars off the road!)

The Self-Cleaning House

Press a button, and soapy water sprays from rotating **nozzles** in the ceiling and cleans the room. Next comes the rinse water. As the water flows toward drains in each corner of the room, hot air blows everything dry. Everything in the room is waterproof or kept inside transparent plastic compartments.

This is not a scene from a movie about the future. It is a description of a room in a real house in the United States in the town of Newberg, Oregon. And there's more. The cupboard where dishes are kept is also a dishwasher, and there's a closet where clothes are washed and dried on hangers. The house's sinks, tubs, and toilets, of course, are all self-cleaning.

The self-cleaning house was invented in the early 1980s by Frances Grace Arnholtz Bateson, who was born in 1915. Frances Gabe, as she is called, is quoted as saying, "Housework is a thankless, unending job....Who wants it? Nobody! With my jaw set hard I was determined there had to be a better way!" She found it. Gabe holds the patents for the devices she invented to clean the house.

It's a mystery why Gabe's invention hasn't become popular—yet. According to the "Inventor of the Week" column published by the Massachusetts Institute of Technology, "It is likely that many of her conveniences, and perhaps even houses modeled on hers, will be adopted for use in time to come." One day, cleaning your room may be as easy as pressing a button—and getting under an umbrella.

Frances Grace Arnholtz Bateson, who calls herself Frances Gabe, hated cleaning —so she did something about it!

Ideas of the Future

Next time you switch on a light, ride your bike, or put on a pair of jeans, think about the inventors of these things—and the stories behind these inventions. Inventors deserve credit for their creativity, originality, and the courage they had to try something new.

You might even invent something of your own. Many young people have. Back in 1991, twelve-year-old Alison DeSmyter invented a portable ramp to help people in wheelchairs (like herself) get over curbs. In 2012, thirteen-year-old Mallory Kievman invented a special lollipop that can cure hiccups. Alison and Mallory are only two of many young inventors.

So if you think you have a good idea—go for it! Get your creativity, originality, and courage working together. You just might come up with the next big invention.

⊣ Tips for Young Inventors ⊢

1. Think of something you'd like to invent—a new device, a game or toy, or even an improvement to something that already exists. Keep a journal of all your ideas. It helps to think of a problem you have, then dream up something that would solve your problem.

2. Make a sketch of what your invention would look like.

3. Explain, in writing, how it would work.

4. Give it a name!

5. Build a model of your invention. Even building it out of cardboard will show you if you need to make changes to your idea. Make your invention the best it can be.

6. Go to the library and check out books for young inventors, or search online for information for young inventors and invention clubs for kids. They will explain how you can patent your idea and get it made for real.

Glossary

archaeologists (ahr-kee-AH-luh-jists) n., scientists who study the past by digging up things made or used by people long ago

banquet (BAN-kwet) n., a fancy meal for a large number of people

commissioned (kuh-MIH-shuhnd) v., paid to do something or create something

concave (kon-KAYV) adj., curved inward, like the inside surface of a bowl

confection (kuhn-FEK-shuhn) n., candy

contraption (kuhn-TRAP-shuhn) n., a strange or odd-looking machine

convex (kon-VEKS) adj., curved outward, like the outside surface of a bowl

dirigible (DIR-uh-juh-buhl) n., a lighter-than-air, cigar-shaped aircraft filled with gas and powered by a motor

filament (FIH-luh-muhnt) n., a very thin wire or thread that glows inside a lightbulb

glider (GLIGH-duhr) n., an aircraft shaped like an airplane that is not powered by an engine but flies by floating and rising on air currents

legendary (LEH-juhn-der-ee) adj., known through stories that are based on fact but may not be entirely true

lens (LENZ) n., a piece of curved glass or plastic that bends light rays to magnify things or make them appear closer

lodestone (LOHD-stohn) n., a stone that contains iron and acts as a magnet

mineral (MIH-nuh-ruhl) n., a solid substance found in nature that comes from rocks or from the ground

navigate (NAH-vuh-gayt) v., to guide a ship or other vehicle so that it does not get lost

nozzle (NAW-zuhl) n., a spout that sprays or directs the flow of liquid

patent (PAH-tuhnt) n., a legal document giving an inventor of an item the right to manufacture or sell that item, and preventing anyone else from doing so

pedestrian (puh-DES-tree-uhn) n., a person who is walking

primitive (PRIH-muh-tiv) adj., simple or crude; like something from long ago

reinforce (ree-uhn-FAWRS) v., to make stronger

rivets (RIH-vuhts) n., metal fastenings that hold cloth or other material together

scholarly (SKAW-luhr-lee) adj., studious, serious, having a great deal of knowledge

shortstop (SHAWRT-stop) n., in baseball, the player who stands between second and third base

Index